A Gu

SURVIVING
THE
STARTUP

WITH YOUR
MIND, BODY & SOUL INTACT

BY HILARY JOHNSON

Cover & Interior Design by Tami Boyce
Photography by Abby Murphy
Edited by Beverly Barfield

ISBN: 0692789588
ISBN-13: 978-0692789582

Pen Paper Pigeon
Charleston, South Carolina

DEDICATION

This book is for you. Yes, you.

You, the girl with a dream of running her own epic business.

You, the girl who actually has the guts to go after her dreams.

You, the girl who turns left when everyone else goes right.

You, the girl who loves a good challenge.

You, the girl who faces her fears with courage.

You, the girl who makes shit happen.

You, the girl who loves her work so much she just might be a little
   crazy.

You, the girl who couldn't go to her deathbed without launching
   this baby.

You, the girl who knows deep within she's capable of greatness.

You, the badass entrepreneur in the making.

Hannah - Keep doing it, girlfriend! you are leading the way for women entrepreneurs everywhere. xo ♡ Hilary

FOREWORD

Not that long ago, I was standing in your shoes. Just like you, I was a girl who had a dream of stepping out on my own, launching a business, and calling my own shots.

And I did it.

It wasn't a decision that came easily and it definitely hasn't been a cakewalk. It has, however, been the most important and meaningful decision I've ever made for my life. Despite facing challenges, financial missteps, and failures of all shapes and sizes, I don't regret for one minute choosing to become an entrepreneur.

I wasn't the obvious choice for an entrepreneur. I was born to two parents who greatly valued stability and being able to provide for their daughter. My mother worked part time for most of my life, which meant she was always there for me at the drop of a hat. She carted me from one side of town to the other, typically for dance classes and social outings, without complaining (at least not out loud) for a second.

Meanwhile, my father devoted over thirty years of his life to one company, climbing the corporate ladder and taking on progressively bigger roles. He often traveled internationally with work, which I thought was super cool. He'd bring back fun trinkets from across the globe, like candy, magazines, and beautiful colored currency that put the U.S. dollar to shame.

My parents were, and still are, exceptional providers in every sense of the word, and I'm extremely grateful for them — but entrepreneurs they were not.

So when, as a 24-year old, I landed a sweet corporate gig working for Miller Brewing Co., my parents were elated. I had a great salary, a corporate car, paid benefits, and all the bells and whistles that came with working in the beer business. I had access to all the free beer I could drink, tickets to NFL games and rock concerts, and VIP access to every bar in Tampa. It was a dream job for a twentysomething.

Turns out I was damn good at my job, and it didn't take long for the higher-ups to notice. During the eight years that followed, I was promoted five times, relocating from Tampa to Montgomery, Alabama to New Orleans to Nashville, and eventually to corporate headquarters in Chicago. I worked in a variety of sales and marketing roles, until I finally landed as the Sports Marketing Manager running the NASCAR sponsorships for Miller Lite and Coors Light.

It was a big job. I was bringing in six figures, living in arguably one of the best cities in the world (despite the fact it's freezing half the year), and traveling across the country to sporting events where "VIP access" was an understatement.

I'm not telling you this to brag. Quite the opposite.

Everyone coveted my job … and I hated it.

When people would learn what I did for a living, they'd proclaim "Wow, what an awesome job you have!" It was all I could do to not roll my eyes. I shut down almost immediately and did anything I could to steer the conversation away from work.

My heart just wasn't in the job, and I felt it in every bone of my body. I was watching my life methodically become someone else's.

I had punched my ticket on the corporate career train, and I found myself enraptured with the idea of making more and more money. Yet, with every relocation or promotion, I was giving away my life. Since I moved every few years, I couldn't put down roots or have meaningful, long-lasting relationships. Because I traveled for work every other week, I had little time to spend with friends (or to even make them!). When I was putting in 12 hours a day for someone else, I came home exhausted, with little energy left to give to my own pursuits.

I was betraying myself by not pursuing the dream buried in my heart: the dream of owning a business and calling my own shots.

It didn't take more than a few months into my first Chicago winter before I figured out that 1) Chicago was absolutely not for this Southern girl; and 2) I needed to get out of there and go after my own darn dreams.

Enough was enough!

I had exactly 24 months on my relocation agreement with my employer. Essentially, if I left before those two years were over, I would have to repay the money the company had paid to move me to Chicago. That wasn't going to happen, so I decided then and there that I would be ready to leave to launch my business at precisely the two-year mark.

And that's what I did.

Every night for almost two years, I moonlighted as a future entrepreneur. I filled notebooks full of business ideas, dreams and possibilities. I gave myself permission to fantasize about a different life.

My lists ran the gamut: open a marketing agency, launch a promotional staffing firm, go back to school to become a photographer, become a yoga teacher, open a bed and breakfast in a hacienda in Mexico. I was all over the place. It was time to reel in my entrepreneurial aspirations and build a viable business plan.

While I was dreaming up business ideas, I was socking away money. When you're coming home every night after work and planning a business, you basically have no social life. I became a bit of a hermit, but I was saving money like a champ. I was also eating pasta and drinking a lot of red wine alone. But somehow it all worked out.

Fast forward to September 30, 2011. It was a day just like any other. I rode the L in to work, walked past the Sears Tower, and took the elevator up to the ninth floor. I got a cup of coffee and made my way to my cubicle. When my boss arrived about 15 minutes later, it felt like it had been an hour. I went to the bathroom and faced myself in the mirror.

"Are you seriously going to do this?" I asked myself aloud.

"Yes — are you freaking kidding me?!" I screamed back.

I slapped my face, as if to jolt myself into action. "Go do it!" I insisted.

I walked out of the bathroom, straight to my boss's cubicle, and asked if I could have a few minutes to chat with him privately. And in the next 10 minutes I would have one of the most pivotal conversations in my life. I resigned from an eight-year career and leapt full force into entrepreneurship.

Thirty days later I took a one-way flight from Chicago to Charleston, S.C., and launched Gusto Group, an event marketing and production firm inspired by my time in the beer business. At MillerCoors, I had worked directly with dozens of top festivals as part of our sponsorship marketing efforts. This gave me an understanding of event planning, production, and partnerships, as well as the logistics on the ground. I saw Gusto Group as being the perfect marriage of my knowledge of events with my ability to plan and organize.

We specialize in creating and developing events from the ground up. We handle everything: concept creation, event planning, marketing, sponsorship sales and day-of production. During our first year of business we launched three giant public festivals, including Charleston Beer Garden — a beer festival, of course!

The event business is not for the faint of heart, as I found out when I was deep in the trenches. The first Spring Jam Music Fest we ever held was a two-day event and we got "lucky" enough to have rain both days. The site was flooded the second day and our headliner's manager was ready to cancel his performance because the stage was partially underwater. But thanks to a persistent production crew and boatloads of mops, buckets, and towels, we found a way to make it happen.

And I still lost $30,000 in a single day. I thought I'd die.

But I rallied, like entrepreneurs do. I reworked my business plan and recommitted, setting a different path forward. During the years that followed, I experienced great successes and other fun failures (aka learning lessons). I'd screw stuff up, and then come up with a solution. I'd second-guess decisions (and third- … and fourth-), and then I'd find the courage to move on. That's Entrepreneurship 101. It's what we do.

Gusto Group became known for producing great events and marketing them like a champ, which parlayed itself into consulting gigs for other events around town. Later, I joined my love of yoga with my experience with events to create YOGAPOP, a yoga and music festival that brought together over 500 people for the largest yoga class Charleston has ever experienced. My business grew and evolved, one step — one decision — at a time.

And now I find myself here, writing this book and launching Hatch Tribe.

Why? Because I want to cultivate a global community of women entrepreneurs who are hell-bent on building one another up and supporting one another's journey.

When I started my business in 2011, I didn't know a single female entrepreneur. I was ill-prepared for the sense of isolation, loneliness, self-doubt, and anxiety that hits so many entrepreneurs over the head. I wanted and needed to know that many of the challenges I was facing were just part of the journey, but I didn't yet have the peers or role models in my circle to tell me so.

So this book is my gift to you, the budding entrepreneur. It's chock-full of lessons I've learned over the years that may help you survive your own startup with your mind, body, and soul intact. Take what works for you and leave the rest behind, because gosh knows there's no one-size-fits-all approach to being a badass boss lady.

I hope this book is a resource when you need a bit of friendly advice and want to know that you're not alone.

You are not alone.

We were all startups once!

(And many of us will do it again and again!)

Becoming an entrepreneur has a way of growing you in ways you never could have known possible. It's epic in every sense of the word. Enjoy the experience, even if you wind up with a few battle scars along the way. At least you'll have a good story to tell, right?!

I'm proud of you. I'm proud of you for following your dreams, for putting ideas into action, and for being a part of a growing community of women who believe in building one another up.

Rock on, girlfriend.

~ Hilary / Hatch Tribe / Founder

SHE BELIEVED
SHE COULD. SO
SHE DID

YOU WILL WORK HARDER THAN YOU EVER HAVE AND YOU WILL LOVE IT

Running your own business is tough! You'll give it your everything: hours, energy, effort, resources, commitment, and boundless love. There will be days when the words "I'm exhausted" don't even begin to describe how you feel.

And yet, owning a business will also be one of the single most rewarding and enlightening experiences you'll ever have. Your hard work will be met with a deep sense of accomplishment and meaning that was simply impossible when you were working for someone else.

The entrepreneurial fire has been lit. Let it burn brightly in your heart.

ONE SIZE DOES NOT FIT ALL

There is no one way to be an entrepreneur. There is no magical formula for success, either.

Plenty of well-intentioned people, including business advisors, may give you advice that leads you in a particular direction that worked perfectly for them in their own circumstances; but that doesn't necessarily mean it's right for you.

Even reading this book — you may love some of these tidbits and hate others. Amen. I hope you do. Because ultimately what I desire for you is that you'll uncover your own unique style and go-to-market strategy that keep you engaged and in love with your business.

Throughout the years I've met countless successful entrepreneurs, and not one of them works just like me. That's freeing in a way, because it means there is no "right way" or "wrong way" to run a business.

Simply be open to the possibilities and be honest with yourself about what's working and what's not. There are a million iterations of success, so create your own.

FEAR IS NOT THE ENEMY

The fear of failure is one of the most common concerns of the budding entrepreneur. And it makes sense: You're leaving behind a comfortable, known existence to embark upon a dream that may or may not work out.

So often I hear the phrase "live fearlessly," and I wonder if that's even possible — or advisable. The fear emotion sits deep within the human makeup. It's basically there to protect us from doing dumb shit. So I'm glad fear kicks in before I do something like jump into a shark tank and try to go for a swim.

However, fear sometimes prevents us from taking action on things that are far less catastrophic than becoming shark bait, such as launching a business or creating a new product.

Fear shouldn't interfere with your ability to take a calculated risk. If you've done your research before making a big decision, you may experience feelings of fear, but by trusting the process and having a little blind faith, you'll find the strength to move forward.

As with all things, you'll never know the outcome unless you give it a try. These days, the fear of regret is far more powerful for me than the fear of failure. So let fear play its role, but you also get busy playing yours, making smart decisions in the face of fear.

YOU WILL MAKE A BOATLOAD OF MISTAKES

I have a little newsflash for you: You're going to make lots of mistakes as an entrepreneur. It's completely irrational to think that you'll run a business (or any endeavor for that matter) and never screw up.

So if you need permission to let loose of your perfectionist tendencies and to fail a time or two, consider it granted.

I, Hilary Johnson, hereby give you permission to make mistakes, screw up, fail, blunder, have an accident, and do some awesomely dumb stuff.

We learn far more from our failures than we do from our successes. When we experience failure we're forced to dig deeply into what happened, consider the steps that got us there, get humble, rework our path forward, and step back into the world with a fresh perspective. It's these times that shape who we are and who we will become.

So relish in the experience of your mistakes and use them as an opportunity to grow. The joy of failure is epic learning.

GIVE UP PUNCHING THE CLOCK

The mandatory 9-to-5 is gone. Bid it adieu!

But as you now find yourself logging well over 40 hours a week growing your business, it's time to start experimenting and developing a schedule that's the perfect fit for you.

Do you thrive working within the structure of a 9-to-5? Do you create your best work bright and early? Are you a night owl who gets super creative once the sun goes down?

How can you take advantage your own natural rhythm to build a schedule that allows you to be at your best throughout the day?

There's no master formula. I've found through the years that experimenting with my schedule has helped me home in on what works best. So play with it, see what works, and ditch the rest.

It's your time now, so make it work best for you!

LEISURE TIME TAKES ON A WHOLE NEW MEANING

The days of watching a "Friends" rerun marathon, reading US Weekly, spending hours shopping for shoes, and drinking a bottle of wine on a Wednesday night have come to an end.

Why? Because your time is super valuable now, and how you choose to spend it is really important.

When you're running a kick-ass business, your free time takes on new meaning and importance. The things you used to love doing may feel trivial and like a waste of time.

But let's be clear: Don't banish all of those amazing diversions. You are still a human being who can't (and shouldn't) work 24 hours a day. You need to have legit leisure in your life!

Prioritize the activities you love that help you feel "whole," and set aside the rest. That may mean saying yes to a quiet dinner out with your besties, instead of a two-hour happy hour, because you want to feel amazing for work the following morning.

The good news is that those "Friends" reruns will be right there waiting for you when you need a mental retreat.

DON'T FORGET YOUR FRIENDS

Your business will become your obsession. It's like having a giant crush on a new boy-toy and wanting to spend every waking moment with him. But I think we all know that scenario almost never plays out well.

Keep your friendships alive. Make it a priority to stay in touch with your friends, whether they're local or out of town. These beautiful souls are the people who have walked beside you and who will continue to support your journey.

Sure, you probably won't be tearing up the town every night, but seeing your best buds will keep you sane. Whether it's meeting up for brunch or grabbing a glass of wine on your friend's couch, take the time to connect and be a good friend. Just like the old days.

PARENTS JUST DON'T UNDERSTAND

Your parents may not get what you're up to. Many of our parents took the "safe route," choosing to work for one or two companies for the length of their careers. They put a high value on things like a steady paycheck, company-paid benefits, and a pension.

So when you try to explain what you're doing, they may not be able to fathom why you'd go out on your own. It seems volatile and unpredictable, and they worry about whether you'll make it financially (or whether you'll come crawling home and ask to live in your old bedroom again).

I was terrified of telling my parents. I imagined that my father was going to look at me with a deeply furrowed brow and tell me I was crazy to give up such a great job. I imagined that my mother was going to be more receptive but that I'd get a cursory "That's great honey," and then she'd tell me everything was going to be ok.

But I got lucky. My parents wound up being supportive beyond belief, even though they've never had any experience running businesses of their own. Their understanding of an entrepreneur's life is limited, but their love for me and support for what I'm creating is boundless.

I'd advise you to appreciate whatever role your parents (or your friends) are capable of playing. If they have firsthand entrepreneurial experience, awesome! Lean on them. If they don't, it's all good. You will find mentors and peers who deeply understand what you're going through. So cut your parents some slack if they worry about you, all right?!

BUILD YOUR TRIBE

When I started my first company, I knew all of three entrepreneurs: my web designer, my production manager, and my event rentals supplier. And they were all dudes.

Talk about a lack of community! I knew there had to be other entrepreneurs — men or women — but where were they hiding?

Frankly, being an entrepreneur can be isolating and lonely. That's why building a community of like-minded friends and business owners can be important for your success and your sanity.

Build your tribe. Look for business owners in your industry and beyond and build a network of peers. Find local meet-up groups and networking functions and look for fellow boss babes to connect with. Uncover ways to help support one another. You'll find most people will be generally supportive — and if they're not, just move on with no hard feelings.

When you find your tribe, your so-called soul sisters, you'll know.

YOUR VIBE ATTRACTS **YOUR TRIBE**

MENTORS COME IN ALL SHAPES AND SIZES

One of the best ways to survive the startup is with an advocate, such as a mentor or a coach, who deeply understands the journey of an entrepreneur.

Mentors come in all forms. It's wonderful to have a mentor from your same industry, as they can help you navigate challenges specific to your business. Just as important, however, are mentors who are simply badass business owners. They'll help you see the bigger picture and weather the storms that are universal across all industries.

Some mentor relationships are formal ("Hey, will you mentor me?") and others are informal and have come together over time. One of my most meaningful mentorships is with a peer, and it's a reciprocal one. I've mentored her and she's mentored me, and we have a profound respect for each other.

Coaches are another wonderful resource for staying on track. You may choose to work with a business coach, who can help you dig into your work, or a personal coach, who will dig in on the mental and emotional side of the journey.

Bottom line: Don't go it alone! Build your own personal "board of directors" and check in with them when you need some help.

So where do you find good mentors? They're everywhere! Whom have you met in your industry that you really admire?

Have you joined a local meet-up for entrepreneurs? Have you connected with Hatch Tribe? We're here for you!

HAVE YOUR SOUL SISTERS ON SPEED DIAL

Hit a rough patch? Worried about whether you're doing the right thing? Feeling like you want to go back to your old job?

Keep the biggest cheerleaders and mentors of your entrepreneurial life close by, and use them. It's what they're there for.

If you can see you're headed into the downward spiral of doubt, hit the pause button and phone a friend. Your soul sisters will cheer you on, and they'll remind you why you chose this path to begin with. Importantly, they'll understand deeply what you're going through, and they'll be able to relate.

Lean on them now, and be there to return the favor later.

ASK FOR HELP

Oh my, how so many of us struggle with this one! So often as entrepreneurs we try to do everything on our own.

It goes something like this: At work you're trying to simultaneously build a website, craft a marketing plan, set up accounting software, and deal with Wi-Fi router issues.

Meanwhile, at home, you're attempting to cook a dish for supper club, walk the dog, clean the toilets, and fix that pesky table leg that's never been level with the floor.

And you wonder why you're overwhelmed and can't get anything done on your biggest work project — which, coincidentally, is none of the things listed above.

Stop the madness! Ask for help. Whether you hire a pro (such as a bookkeeper) or a friend (your gal pal will totally walk your dog), you'll get back some sanity right away and free up time to focus on your most important work.

You'll also be surprised how many friends and family members are willing to pitch in to help you succeed. If you're worried you might be inconveniencing people by asking for help, remember they always have the right to say no.

It takes a village to raise a business. Ask for help, boss babe!

IT'S A SMALL, SMALL WORLD

This lesson is plain and simple. Don't be an asshole and don't burn bridges. The world is just way too small.

It doesn't seem to matter how big of a city you live in. Or how big of an industry you work in. The same people tend to stay in orbit and will keep popping up over time, but often in different companies or roles.

The person you're a jerk to today could very well be in a capacity to make or break a business deal for you later. And frankly, no one likes a raging bitch anyway, so it's best to keep that alter ego out of business dealings.

YOU'RE GONNA SUCK AT SOMETHING

You're a badass boss lady. I know it. You know it. Your friends and colleagues know it.

But you are not great at everything. And part of being a strong leader is acknowledging and accepting what you suck at, so you can get the help you need and deserve.

Some things are simply best done by others who may be more knowledgeable, or faster, or have more time than you do currently. And that's A-OK! You want to surround yourself with a team of talented individuals who make up for your shortfalls and build you up.

You don't need to be a superhero. You don't need to be a master of everything. You do need to know your limitations and find someone to lend a hand. You'll save your business a ton of time, money, and opportunity costs. It's a true sign of strength when you ask for help.

GOODBYE, PROBLEMS HELLO, SOLUTIONS

What people don't tell you when you're starting a business is that you'll be getting a doctorate in problem-solving. So much of what we do as entrepreneurs is built around our ability to recognize a problem and find a solution.

This is likely the cornerstone of your business. You saw a problem that you could help solve with a product or service, and you set out to create it. Boom!

But the problem-solving goes well beyond what you're selling. It becomes part of the essence of how you operate as an entrepreneur. Gone are the days when you could sit back and point to everything that was wrong and hope someone else would fix it.

That type of thinking is rampant in corporate offices and traditional employment. I observed this on the daily in my corporate job, as my co-workers would point out many things that needed to be fixed but then would quickly back away and say it wasn't their job or within their capacity to do anything about it.

Being the boss lady you are, you don't have time for this. When you see something that needs to be fixed, you're in solution mode in no time flat. It might be something as stupid as fixing your office printer that keeps eating paper. Or it might be something as big as updating your company's app to fix bugs from the first iteration.

There's no time for bitching and moaning. Solutions are the name of your game.

STOP COMPLAINING ALREADY

First off, complaining is super unattractive. When was the last time you sat on the receiving end of an onslaught of complaints and thought, "Wow, I am just loving this conversation"? So give your teammates and friends a few hours of their life back.

Second, remember that you're now in the solutions business. On the surface it might feel good to complain and get it off your chest, but more often than not, complaining just makes the story bigger, more powerful, and more painful.

Plenty of things in business will not go as planned, and it will tick you off. And you may feel a little complaining is justified. I'm just going to ask you to limit the amount of time you stay in the grumble zone. The quicker you move into solution mode, the less time you spend complaining.

A MASTERS IN EVERYTHING

One minute you're trying to figure out how to build your own website, to save money; the next minute you're trying to fix the corrupted hard drive on your computer. Two days later when your production line runs amok, you're on it like a moth to a flame.

The job of an entrepreneur is multifaceted and seemingly never-ending. You'll tackle the biggest and the smallest of issues, and everything in between, because when you're bootstrapping a startup there is no job that's beneath you.

I like to think of this time as the best learning I ever received. You grow more in one year as an entrepreneur than you do in four years of college. Guaranteed.

Simply put: Best. Degree. Ever.

EXPLOIT THE DAYLIGHTS OUT OF YOUR STRENGTHS

It pays to know what you're good at, because if you spend your time leveraging your strengths, you'll deliver big value for your business.

Are you a rock-star web designer but terrible at handling the books? Do you excel in product innovation but can't create a beautiful client presentation to save your life? Do you love engaging with your customers on social media, but packing and shipping products makes you cringe?

Whatever you rock at, lean into it. When you operate from your zone of excellence (and passion), you'll create your best work, enjoy the process, and drive profits for your business in the most meaningful way.

Meanwhile, whatever you suck at, find a solution for it. That might mean hiring someone to help or getting some education so you can improve your own skills.

The key is to be honest with yourself. Own your truth.

PLAN TO KNOCK IT OUT OF THE PARK

My very first boss, Tony, introduced to me this concept: "If you fail to plan, you plan to fail." This wisdom has been passed down over the ages, through countless businesses and millions of talented minds. Why? Because it's tried and true.

If you start your day with a very clear plan of what needs to happen and how it's going to get done, you've created a roadmap for success. You just have to execute it.

Conversely, if you don't have a plan, you may find yourself just wandering aimlessly through work. Sure, you might have been busy answering all those emails, making phone calls, and catching up on miscellaneous to-do's, but did you actually accomplish anything meaningful?

When we set a plan for how we'll allocate our time, we can methodically and consistently make progress against our goals. You'll be moving the ball forward versus just kicking it around the field.

Become a planning and executing machine and you'll knock it out of the park!

WHAT WOULD YOU DO IF YOU KNEW YOU COULD NOT FAIL?

CREATE A WORKSPACE
THAT INSPIRES YOU

You're going to be spending a lot of time at work, so it's important to create an environment that enables you to be at your best. Whether you work from home or go in to an office, consider how you function best and what will delight and inspire you every day.

If you love bright, airy spaces with minimalist design, your office will look and feel a lot different from that of the girl boss who loves a cozy feel with oversized furnishings and a giant library of books. Neither is right or wrong, it's simply about creating a space that inspires you. Pinterest can be a wonderful resource for finding images of inspiring workspaces.

I like to have a few live plants in my office because it brings an element of fresh air and vibrancy to the space. I also like little elements that remind me of my friends and family. It helps me stay motivated and remember who I am in my heart when I'm having a tough day at the office.

Whatever lights you up, find a way to incorporate it into your field of vision. It makes a world of difference!

GET ORGANIZED

am a stickler for organization, so I'm biased. But having worked with my fair share of disorganized business owners, I can attest that it only creates more stress. The inability to quickly find important information, documents, or files wastes time and energy.

Adopt a system for your life and office that keeps you on track. Here are three tips I've found to be incredibly helpful over the years:

Take handwritten notes in only one place. Whether it's a bound notebook, legal pad, or loose-leaf paper, choose one and stick with it for your daily notes, rather than having it scattered everywhere.

Create a digital filing system that mirrors how you break down your work. Use folders to group files that belong together. For example, you may have a folder for each client you work with (Client A, Client B, Client C). And within each client's folder you'll create a series of other folders (Invoices, Contracts, Presentations, Logos, etc.).

Process your paperwork. What does this mean? It means your notes, invoices, bills, handouts, etc. shouldn't sit around forever in your inbox or desktop. Processing moves items from "pending" to "complete." For example, archive your email after you read and respond. Mark bills as "paid" when complete and move them into a binder. Review your handwritten notes regularly and check off action items as they are complete.

There's no secret trick to getting organized, but I encourage you to try things on and see what works for you. When you have a system in place it becomes automatic, which means you can free up vital brain space to focus on other things — like landing that next big client!

YOU DO NOT NEED A FAX MACHINE

Enough said.

WRITE IT DOWN

Experts estimate that the human brain experiences 50,000 to 70,000 thoughts per day, which means that in a single hour you could have nearly 3,000 things floating through that head of yours. For an entrepreneur, that's potentially hundreds of new ideas and tidbits for your business in any given day.

How many of those thoughts will you actually remember to-morrow? A fraction.

Sure, they're not all life-changing, world-altering thoughts, but hidden within your stream of consciousness will be daily gems.

So if you're the type of gal who never writes anything down, it's time to start! Keep a notebook (or use your cellphone) to capture those nuggets of genius before they're gone.

MONTHLY "CEO SESSIONS" ARE A MUST

I want you to pull out your calendar right now and schedule one full day each month for a "CEO Session."

The idea is to devote one day each month to thinking about the big picture of your business. It's time to shut down the email and to-do lists, so you can focus on the bigger vision for your company.

Start by taking an honest look at the current state of your business. Ask yourself the following questions and then add your own:

- How is my business performing?
- Am I meeting my goals?

- What's working?
- What's not?
- How is my team performing?

Capture the answers in writing.

Then look ahead at the next six months. What are the goals you've set for your business during that time frame? If you didn't set any before, now's a great time to do it. And if any of those goals no longer feels appropriate or if they need to be tweaked, go for it!

Then I want you to think about how that work will be accomplished during those next six months. What is the work you are personally taking on? What is being assigned to your team? Do you need to hire anyone — internal or outsourced — to help you accomplish those goals? Are there any issues you need to address in the coming months based on the current state of your business? Build a clear plan of what's to be accomplished in the next month, who's responsible, and what's the timeline.

The final part of the CEO Session is rolling out your monthly plan to your team. Think of it as a kickoff for the work that lies ahead. This can be a great time to gather your team in person (if logistics permit) and get everyone rallied for the cause. A little celebration doesn't hurt either, so take this time to acknowledge the wins you've had as a team.

When we regularly step away from the daily burn of work to focus on the bigger picture, we can stay tuned in to our mission, vision, and goals. It's a commitment of time that pays dividends in keeping you focused on what's important.

PRIORITIZE

f you've never read the "Seven Habits of Highly Effective People" by Stephen Covey, stop what you're doing and order it now. It's a must-read for entrepreneurs who are looking to maximize their time and energy.

Habit No. 3 is "Put first things first."

This concept is about prioritizing your work by putting the things that are of the most value and worth first.

Put simply, you should:

- Spend the majority of your time working on the stuff that matters.
- Minimize the time you spend working on the crap that drives little value to your business (think minimize, delegate, or outsource)

If you put first things first, you'll be a goal-crushing machine in no time!

JUST SAY NO

You need to get comfortable with saying no.

This is a skill some of you may already have mastered. And to you, I offer a giant high-five!

But for many of you, especially my "people-pleasing" friends, you may find this a true challenge. You may feel bad for telling someone no, even when you end up causing harm or inconveniencing yourself by saying yes.

There is an art and skill to saying no, but this is why it's important that you become comfortable with the practice. As a business owner, you simply do not have enough time, money, or bandwidth to say yes to everything. You need to make choices and prioritize.

This means you may say no to some customer requests because they're too time-consuming and cut into your profits, but you say yes to the ones that make the most sense for your business and are mutually beneficial.

This means you may say no to half of the meeting requests that come your way because there are only so many times you can "let someone pick your brain," but you will say yes to those handful of quality new introductions that you're really jazzed about.

This means you may say no to some charities that ask you to donate an item to their auction, but you will say yes to the handful of causes you truly want to support with your in-kind donation.

You can say no and do so thoughtfully and with finesse. Be polite, but firm. Resist the urge to apologize profusely. A simple, "I'm sorry," followed by a brief explanation of why you are saying no, is sufficient. It doesn't make you a jerk. It does, however, make you a hell of a business owner who knows how to prioritize and protect her valuable time and resources.

GUARD YOUR TIME

When you own a business, people come out of the woodwork wanting to chat about what you do, to sell you their services, pick your brain, or otherwise "steal" an hour of your time for coffee or lunch.

While many meetings will be important and productive, if you take every meeting that comes your way, you will never have enough time to run your business or focus on your most important work.

Over the years I've found it helpful to answer a few questions before taking meetings.

- Are both parties clear on the objectives for the meeting?
- Will this meeting be mutually beneficial?

- Are you excited about meeting with this person to discuss this topic?

If the answer is yes to all, rock on sister! If it's not, reconsider. Say no to meetings that aren't the best use of your time and resources. Whether you flat-out reject the meeting or choose to take a quick 15-minute phone call instead, don't feel bad about saying no. Your time is your most valuable resource, boss babe, so just say no with kindness and respect and get back to kicking butt at work!

END WITH THE BEGINNING IN MIND

You've probably heard of the idea of "beginning with the end in mind." Often we use this approach when we're setting goals because it's helpful to have a vision of where you're headed. It allows you to create a clear path that leads you to a desired outcome. And it's an excellent approach.

Now, I'd like to flip this statement on its head. Let's "end with the beginning in mind."

So much of our time ends up wasted when we're "preparing to work": You've arrived at work in the morning and you're not exactly sure what to start on. So maybe you check some emails, review your calendar for the week, and organize some papers on your desk. And then you think about the things you need to do, so you create a little (or massive) to-do list. Before you know it, an hour of your time is gone and you've basically done nothing.

If you want to hit the ground running every single day, it all starts the day before as you "end with the beginning in mind."

Make it a habit to spend the final 15 minutes of your workday creating a plan of action for the following day. Review your schedule, recap your to-do list, prioritize your top projects, and then schedule those projects into your calendar. Be decisive about what you can actually get done, and prioritize those mission-critical projects.

Now when you arrive at work, you can just get started. Right away. No more lollygagging, sister; you are one well-oiled machine!

DO SOMETHING
TODAY
THAT YOUR
FUTURE SELF WILL
THANK YOU FOR

DON'T FALL DOWN THE EMAIL RABBIT HOLE

There was a time when hearing the words "You've got mail" from your AOL account was super exciting. Now, our inboxes are bombarded with hundreds of messages daily, and it's a chore to deal with it all.

Many companies are experimenting with eliminating email or at least limiting the hours it's available to their employees, to end this compulsion to be connected and responding at all times.

You might not be ready to give up email cold turkey, but remember that email is just another form of communication, like the telephone or a live meeting. Email does not equal work.

Create boundaries around email. It's good for your productivity — and sanity! Start by establishing specific windows of time when you will tackle email. For example, you might set aside 30 minutes midmorning and 30 minutes at the end of the day. During this time, you'll focus exclusively on processing your email (replying, deleting, marking as spam, archiving, etc.)

Choose what requires an email reply and what's better-suited for a conversation. If you can handle it with a quick phone call and shorten the exchange, go for it. If you can walk a few desks down and chat it out with your team, you must.

If you choose to reply via email, keep it short, sweet, and concise. And always remember fewer emails out = fewer emails in.

As for the rest of the day, keep your email off! Turn off notifications and stop checking your phone like an obsessed teenager so you can work on the really important stuff.

SHUT THE COMPUTER OFF RIGHT NOW, SISTER

As all-consuming as your work can be, it's important to remember to shut the computer down and step away. Life doesn't happen only at work and behind our desks.

Shut down, power off, and recharge so you can crush it the next day. Remember, you're it in for the long haul, not a sprint.

A fellow entrepreneur friend shared that she and her husband have a "no computer" rule after 9 at night. They give themselves permission to work up until 9 p.m., but then it's time to power down. They spend the rest of the night reconnecting with each other, live and in color, without any distractions. She insists it has kept their marriage intact through years of launching and running businesses.

Set your own boundaries so you'll have time to spend with all the other amazing people and things in your life that matter.

UNPLUG EVERYTHING

What if you carved out one day every single week to be completely unplugged?

No computer. No telephone. No TV. No iPad. No iPod. No nada.

We're in a new era, one of technology and information over-load. And most of us are glued to our devices more than we'd care to admit. I can't tell you how many times I've found myself check-ing Instagram within minutes of waking up. I know better and yet I can't resist it sometimes. Addicted to technology? Maybe.

This doesn't even scratch the surface of what's happening in public. How often have you seen entire tables of people in a restaurant jamming away on their phones and not talking to one another? It's everywhere, and I'm just as guilty as the next gal of doing this at times.

Isn't it amazing, though, when we just put down our phones and engage in some human-to-human conversation — you know, actually looking at each other in the eyes when we're speaking? Or when we take the time to simply enjoy walking around the neighborhood, taking in the sights and sounds of nature in its glory, without feeling compelled to listen to a podcast at the same time?

I encourage you to start by carving out one hour every sin-gle day to be unplugged. I enjoy making this the last hour of my day, as it gives my mind time to unwind and helps me get ready for bed.

Then start upping the ante so you can work toward an entire day unplugged. Sound insane? Start with Sunday mornings from 8 a.m. to noon. Fill up that time with quality experiences, whether it's spending time with family and friends or taking time alone to read a book or walk the dog. Let your brain recharge. You'll come back so refreshed on Monday, you'll be raring to go!

TAKE CARE OF YOURSELF

This isn't just lip service, ladies. More than ever before, your self-care is critical. As you devote countless hours to your business, your own self-care may get pushed to the back burner.

If there's one thing I've learned over the years, it's that I am at my best at work when I am engaged in regular self-care: exercising, eating well, and taking some time to disconnect and decompress.

Make time every day, even if it's just 30 minutes, to go for a jog, do some yoga, or join a friend for a spin class. Physical activity shifts energy in the body, giving your brain time to recharge.

Eat well. Fill up your day with real, whole foods like fruits, vegetables, nuts, and whole grains. Skip the empty calories that spike your energy but then send you into a crash so severe you need a nap. Goodbye, doughnut. Hello, apple!

Your body is your temple. Treat it as such and it will reward you with a foundation that allows you to tackle your work head-on. A strong body fuels a strong mind.

MASTER THE MINI BREAK

Working nonstop is bad for your body and brain, to say nothing of the quality of work you're producing.

Make it your mission to step away from your work every two hours, giving yourself 15-20 minutes of work- and technology-free time.

Leave your computer and phone behind. This is not the time to check Facebook, answer personal emails, shop Etsy online, or play Angry Birds on your phone.

The goal here is to "change lanes." Go for a walk, play with your dog, have a smoothie, sit quietly in meditation, listen to music, take a power nap.

Yes, I said it. Take a power nap if that's what would serve you best in those 15 minutes! Permission granted.

After your mini break, you'll return to your work refreshed and recharged. Go knock it out of the park, girlfriend!

FUEL UP

A girl's got to eat! This might sound like obvious advice, but it's easy to get so caught up in your work that you destroy your good eating habits.

Either you'll find yourself slumped over your computer, mindlessly chowing down on a sandwich, or you'll blow past the hunger phase into "hangry" territory and rip someone's head off before you finally stop to eat.

When you're hungry, your brain literally doesn't have the fuel it needs to produce extraordinary thinking. And when we don't slow down long enough to truly enjoy the meal in front of us, we never really satisfy the hunger within.

Plan your meals ahead. Schedule lunch into your agenda and take a true break from your work, even if it's just 15 minutes. Whether you're dining out or packing a lunch, fill up on fresh, unprocessed, whole foods like fruits, vegetables, and whole grains to give you the long-lasting energy you need.

You're a powerhouse who deserves only the best fuel.

GET YOUR BEAUTY REST

Sleep is oh-so-necessary for the entrepreneur. If you're going to run a business like a champ, your brain and body need sleep. It takes a lot of energy to get up every day and do what we do.

There will be times when sleep will elude you. You'll be too excited to sleep. Or too stressed to sleep. Or just have too much work to sleep. We've all been there. Seek to minimize these occasions.

Prioritize getting seven to eight hours of sleep each night. Shut off all technology at least an hour before bed to give your brain time to relax. It's a great time to take a bath, read, catch up with your partner, or just chill out.

Over the years I've learned that I function best with about seven and a half hours of sleep. I wrap up my night around 10 p.m. with the goal of being asleep by 11 p.m. I set my alarm for 7 a.m., but almost always I wake up at 6:30 a.m. I am one of those sickos who enjoy waking up before their alarm goes off.

So figure out what works best for you and rock it out!

TAKE A SHOWER ALREADY

If you work from home, you may find yourself in the morning jamming away on your laptop, in your pajamas, with dirty hair and unbrushed teeth. You know how gross you are right now.

This is ok every now and again, but let's agree right now to make it a rare occurrence.

When we show up sloppy, we tend to produce sloppy results.

Establish a morning routine that leaves you feeling refreshed, empowered and ready to take on the day. Get up, get showered, and start fresh. This is all about setting the stage for you to produce your best work.

Act the part, boss lady.

DRESS THE PART

When I left my corporate job, I was thrilled to take every single pair of black slacks I owned to Goodwill. Those days are done! Now you'll typically find me wearing a nice pair of jeans with a cute blouse to everything work-related. But that isn't to say that I don't dress up when it's needed.

The key is to know your audience. What is right for your industry, business, clients, and occasion?

If you're in the tech world, everyone around you might be rocking jeans and t-shirts as they code away on their laptops, while an attorney may be rocking tailored suits to court every day. And a women's clothing store owner may find it helps sell clothes when the female staff members wear things from the store.

Think about what your clothing says about you as a business owner. Use common sense and, when in doubt, overdress. And let's all agree that jeans with frayed holes are never appropriate, ok?!

EARLY BIRD OR NIGHT OWL

It pays to know when you do your best work.

You might be the type of person who leaps out of bed before the alarm goes off and is crushing goals before 10 a.m. Rock on!

You might be the type of person who can't wait until the sun goes down, because that's when the juices start flowing and you create epic stuff. Amen!

Neither is right or wrong, it's just who you are. So get to know yourself and when you feel the most energetic and vibrant throughout the day. Schedule your most important projects during those times so you can take advantage of your natural high.

THERE WILL BE SLEEPLESS NIGHTS AND LONG DAYS

've lost count of the number of times I've lay awake in bed at night spinning in a vortex of thoughts. Even with the best meditation and yoga training under my belt, sometimes there simply isn't enough deep breathing to break out of the "monkey mind."

Perhaps you've been there too. Swirling through your brain are good ideas, bad ideas, fearful ideas, and some plain ol' dumb ideas. You'll problem-solve, you'll daydream, you'll cry a bit, and then you'll crazily laugh at the fact that you're still awake. And then, because life can be cruel, you'll nod off to sleep for 30 minutes right before your alarm goes off.

Of course, this is all the while you're putting in well over 40 hours a week at work. Sometimes you just wish you could just come home at 5 p.m. and curl up in your PJs on the couch and watch "Downton Abbey" reruns. Alas, this is not the life you chose! Besides, you quite love your work anyway, even when you are burning the candle at both ends.

Just know that you're not alone. Thousands of other entrepreneurs across the globe are busting their asses by day, chasing their dreams, and going crazy sleepless at night.

I've found that these days and nights come in waves. Just as soon as they arrive, they leave. But if you find this happening more than a few nights a week and your sleep is really suffering, it's time to seek help. Meditation and yoga may be just the thing you need, but consider seeing a doctor or a therapist if you need more. There is no shame in this game. Do what you gotta do, girl.

ALWAYS REMEMBER YOUR WHY

PUT DOWN THE BOTTLE OF WINE

Hey girl, I know it's easy to get carried away and polish off that bottle of Malbec, but take it easy on the drinking.

A hangover on someone else's dime is one thing. You sit back in your desk chair and try to look busy on whatever you're "working on," while you're actually shopping for new shoes online and reading the news.

A hangover on your dime? Stupid. You'll feel like crap as you watch your own precious time dwindle away while fighting off a pounding headache and the urge to puke. You won't be productive, you'll lack clarity of mind, and you'll lose an entire day of work because of your own stupidity.

Keep it in check and make it your mission to be at your best every single day.

OVERWHELM AND EXHAUSTION LIKE TO DOUBLE-DATE

The life of an entrepreneur ain't easy.

You're going to have days when you feel completely overwhelmed and think "Oh my God, my to-do list is 12 miles long!"

And you're going to have days when you feel completely exhausted and wonder "When was the last time I slept through the night without waking up thinking about work?"

It's gonna happen.

For a long time, I would wake up many nights at 2 a.m. Despite knowing better, I'd still roll over and look at my clock, which reconfirmed my suspicions of what time it was. Then my brain would immediately launch into obsessions about work. I'd think about what had gone wrong the day before, what needed to be fixed, and what I was freaking out about for the next day. It's funny how it's rarely lovely thoughts that keep us awake at night. I'd be so jazzed to lie awake thinking about an upcoming vacation instead!

Often I'd lie awake for hours just spinning in the hamster wheel of thoughts, and then manage to fall asleep just before my alarm went off. I'd wake up dead tired and completely overwhelmed thinking about the day ahead.

Overwhelm and exhaustion tend to go hand-in-hand, and it can be tough, so I encourage you to engage in extreme self-care when this happens. It might be time to pick up a meditation practice, take yoga classes, or engage in some deep breathing techniques. Or maybe carving out 30 minutes to take a nap midafternoon can take the edge off. Sometimes it helps to just talk out the problems that are keeping you up at night, so whether you engage a colleague, coach, friend, or a therapist, get it out of your head.

Take it easy on yourself. Remember: This, too, shall pass.

CRY, SCREAM, CURSE

Things will not always go your way. It's part of life.

So when they don't, give yourself permission to have a mini meltdown. It's important to process our emotions and blow off steam. But it's also important to know when to call it quits, so you don't become paralyzed by negative emotions.

I call this the 5-Minute Meltdown. Set the timer on your phone for five minutes and go freaking nuts. Lose your mind, scream, punch a pillow, talk it out, and cry your face off.

(Be sure to do this privately and not in front of your team, ok? You're not trying to scare them to death!)

When the five minutes are over, this pity party is done. Pull up your big-girl pants, wash the sad-clown mascara off your face, and move on.

Be gentle with yourself as you step back into work. With your emotions in check, you'll find it easier to move forward.

You've got this, girlfriend.

DON'T LOSE YOUR SENSE OF HUMOR

Well, of course this assumes you had one in the first place, but I'm going to guess you do.

Running a business can be so serious. You're trying to grow a profitable company while making huge decisions daily and putting in epically long hours. So it's easy for "resting bitch face" to become a part of your regular routine.

But I encourage you to find the silly, lighthearted fun that's always resting just below the surface. Life is way too short to build a company culture that doesn't appreciate some levity.

Laugh at yourself. Make fun of your mistakes. Be a little self-deprecating for the benefit of the team. You'll create a company culture that people can actually enjoy, and that's always a win.

WHERE IS ALL THIS GRAY HAIR COMING FROM

The entrepreneur life is no joke. You'll grow and learn so much that it quite literally will turn your hair gray. It's a little bit like how President Obama's hair (and that of almost every president before him) went from pitch black to mostly salt, no pepper, during his term in office.

I like to stand in the mirror and admire my gray hair. It's my badge of honor. I earned those silver streaks fair and square growing my business.

Then, before I get too attached to them, I immediately schedule a hair appointment so I can return my locks to a rich chocolate brown.

Listen, we're all going to get older. Gray hair, wrinkles, and saggy bits. But the truth is, you've chosen a hell of a way to get there. Be proud of yourself for taking the leap of running your own business. It's a wild ride.

THE HUSTLE IS REAL

You've undoubtedly heard the phrase "The struggle is real." But I invite you to consider a different version for your entrepreneur life.

"The hustle is real."

Let's take a look at these two words according to Merriam-Webster.

- Hustle = "to move or work in a quick and energetic way"
- Struggle = "to move with difficulty or with great effort"

Which one feels more powerful to you? Which life do you want?

The entrepreneur life is all about the hustle. It's vibrant, it's energetic, it's full of motion toward a goal. It's a life of passion and the pursuit of something that feels just beyond your reach. It lights you up.

This is your life now. Embrace it.

BE YOU

You're no longer playing dress-up and going into a job that you only halfway love. You don't have to fake it or try to fit in anymore. This baby is yours.

So make it your mission every day to be you. Let your inner light shine through in everything you do for your company.

Authenticity is the name of this game. Be you, exactly as you are … you beautiful, wild soul.

PUT ON THE KID GLOVES

There will be times when you second- (third- … and fourth-) guess your abilities. Your inner chatter will crank up and tell you things like "you suck at this," or "you're never going to make this successful," or "people are going to think you're so stupid if this fails."

This is fear in action. Our nasty little egos love to beat us up and take us for an emotional ride.

When this happens, I want you to just observe it for a second. Listen to the words playing on this "highlight reel" and then consider for a moment whether you'd ever say those things to another entrepreneur on her journey.

Answer: You would never!

This is when we need put our egos in check. Steer your thoughts toward all of those amazing things that you're capable of and that you do on a daily basis. Do your best to tune out the negativity. It might help to pick up the phone and call a mentor or friend who can help get you out of your head.

Don't beat yourself up when the inner dialogue gets rolling. Just be kind to yourself. You are capable of far more than you know.

THE CURE FOR DOUBT IS ACTION

There will be many times in business where the possibilities seem endless and the solution unclear. While it's wonderful to have the freedom to set your own course for your business, it can also feel incredibly daunting.

As the owner and CEO of your business, many decisions you make will affect the bottom line of your company. Get it right, grow your profits and give yourself a bonus! Get it wrong, you're eating ramen noodles for a few months. This proposition can often lead even the brightest minds to become paralyzed by their options and fail to take action.

When I find myself stuck in a doubt-ridden trap, I begin an experiment to start testing the possibilities. I like to think of it like a seventh-grade science class experiment. There's a question I'd like to solve, so I create a hypothesis and test it. There's something about conjuring up this vision of myself as a 12-year-old that makes it seems way less overwhelming and more like a fun day dissecting a frog.

Try the one thing that "seems" like the best choice and see how it goes. If it feels like it's headed in the wrong direction, you'll make a new choice that will allow you to test a second course of action. And if that doesn't work, you're on to test No. 3. And so on, and so on.

We start replacing doubt when we take action, because each time we test a possibility, we learn more information that better informs our next steps.

Honestly, this is my favorite thing about being an entrepreneur. I love the ability to try something on and see how it goes.

If it sucks, shut it down! If it rocks, let's party! Take action to obliterate your doubt.

TAKE A (BRAIN) DUMP

Hands down this is one of my favorite activities!

When my mind gets super-full of ideas and starts to feel like a hamster running on a wheel, I reach for pen and paper. I set a timer for 30 minutes and I proceed to dump out everything that's on my mind.

I put it all on paper. No matter how small or grand, unrelated or critically important, business or personal. It doesn't matter. I just get it out.

When I'm done (or the 30 minutes are over), I take five minutes to sit quietly and breathe. Then I put the paper in a folder and go back to work.

What I typically find is my mind is no longer racing and I feel good knowing all those thoughts are captured somewhere safe, so that I don't have to actively think about them anymore. This allows me to refocus on my most important work.

Later on, I dig out the list and review it for what's really important. There are typically a few items that rise to the top that need to be acted upon, so I add those to my project list and schedule a time in my calendar to work on them.

Give it a try next time your brain is overflowing.

DO ONE THING

Do you ever find yourself staring at your computer and thinking "OMG, I have so much stuff to do, I don't even know where to start!"?

You are not alone. This is just part of being a business owner.

When your task list seems insurmountable and you're struggling to prioritize, just do one thing. It always feels better to take a step forward, no matter how small it may be. Just do one thing.

It's like your own version of completing a marathon. Just keep putting one foot in front of the other, and the next thing you know you'll have run 26.2 miles. The momentum will build and you'll get back on track before you know it, sister!

DOUBT
KILLS MORE DREAMS
THAN
FAILURE
EVER WILL

DECISION FATIGUE IS REAL

There's a reason Facebook founder Mark Zuckerberg wears a gray t-shirt every day. It's one less decision he has to make, so he can conserve his energy for more important matters.

I'm not suggesting you go crazy and give up your beautiful wardrobe! But there is a lesson in here.

As a business owner, you'll have a string of decisions lined up at your door like customers waiting at the Apple Store for the new iPhone release. The human brain begins each day with a strong capacity for decision-making, but as the day goes on, it becomes fatigued from critical thinking. Your resolve and confidence around big decisions will start to wane as decision fatigue sets in.

So what's a boss lady to do?

Knock out critical decisions early in the day when your brain is fresh! And create systems around the daily decisions that you can control. For example, routine decisions like what to wear and eat for breakfast are ones you can make the night before, so you can start each morning without the brain strain.

CREATE BEFORE YOU CONSUME

I love this concept in action, so try it on for size.

Tomorrow, when you wake up, don't turn on a single piece of technology or consume any media. No morning TV shows, no social media, no emails. Keep the devices powered down.

Your mind is the freshest and purest it will be all day, after a night of restorative sleep. Your brain is untainted by current events, social media, or the words or thoughts of others, so it's an ideal time to focus on your own creation.

Take the next hour to focus on a specific project that requires you to create for your business. It might be brainstorming new ideas for a product, writing a blog post, mapping out a three-year vision for your business, or assembling a mood board for your client.

Let your creative juices flow!

I've found this simple tactic often produces the best work because my mind is free and unburdened. So give it a whirl.

PUT YOUR GOALS FRONT AND CENTER, LITERALLY

Let's take a look at the queen of all goals: the New Year's resolution. Whether you love them or hate them, the beginning of the year is one of the most common times in life that we set big goals for ourselves.

And what percentage of those goals do you think are ever achieved? Studies show it's as little as 8%.

There are many reasons goals don't get met. The SMART philosophy tells us that goals need to be specific, measurable, achievable, realistic, and time-bound.

So maybe you didn't define your goal well enough to create a path to success. Or you may have set a goal that you simply didn't feel passionate about, so it loses its luster after a few weeks.

But often it's a whole other issue and one that's rather simple to solve: It's about the visibility of your goals. I want you to be able to see your goals every single day.

It's easy to get caught up chasing the business. You know, answering emails, digging through bills, invoicing clients, scheduling meetings for your team, and other non-value-added activities. If you spend all your time on these tasks, you never get around to focusing on the important, value-driving part of your business. Put simply, you don't focus on the work necessary to deliver your big goals.

By displaying your goals in a loud and proud manner in your office, you'll face them head-on every single day. I like to put them right in front of my face, thumbtacked to the wall. This forces me to ask myself if the work I'm doing (right now) is contributing to those goals. It's a quick, easy way to constantly check in and stay focused on my most meaningful work.

Goals don't belong buried in a notebook in a box. Let those babies out!

KNOW YOUR CUSTOMER LIKE YOU KNOW YOUR BFF

If there's one thing that builds the foundation of any successful business, it's knowing the customer to whom you are selling. You should know her like the back of your hand.

What kind of person is she? What does she love? What does she hate? What kind of lifestyle does she live? And so on. These traits inform the creation of an avatar, or the description of one ideal customer for your business.

I've found having an avatar in mind to be particularly useful when I'm writing copy for marketing materials. I like to imagine my avatar (her name is Hope) hearing the marketing message and consider what she would think. Would my message resonate with Hope? Would she find it interesting? Am I solving one of her pain points with this offer or message?

If you need help developing an avatar, I highly recommend listening to Amy Porterfield's "Online Marketing Made Easy" podcast. Episode No. 106, with Jasmine Star, is titled "Are You Repelling or Attracting Your Potential Customers?" Check it out on iTunes Podcasts or at her website.

It's also critical to understand your target market. This is a broader definition of your customer base than an avatar, but it's especially important if you're investing in advertising.

Let's look at an example. Here's how a wine bar might define its target market:

- Men and women, skewing 65% women
- Ages 21-65
- Lives within a 10-mile radius of the bar
- Middle to high income levels ($50,000+/year)
- White-collar workers and professionals, with some service industry
- Interests in wine, high-end cocktails (bourbon, scotch), and craft beer
- Lifestyle interests include travel, vineyards, boating, high-end cuisine

The more you understand your customer, the better you can define your target market. Then, when you invest in paid marketing efforts, you can focus on your target market and get the best bang for your buck! You're spending money for the right customer to hear your message, versus throwing it out into an undefined sea of people and hoping it resonates with someone.

DEVELOP SUPERPOWER LISTENING SKILLS

The Greek philosopher Epictetus said, "We have two ears and one mouth so that we can listen twice as much as we speak."

Girl, let me tell you how much I've struggled with this one! I've had the gift of gab for as long as I can remember, so I often struggle to balance speaking with listening.

But this funny thing happens when you shut up. You actually start hearing cues that help you become a better boss, a better friend, a better girlfriend/wife, a better daughter ... basically a better human.

It's time to develop superhuman listening skills. People will tell you what they need. In business, your customers and clients will give you great insight into your products or services. They provide priceless information that will help you improve your offerings and drive more sales. You just have to listen.

Treat your customers like your best friend. Listen to them with your head ... and your heart.

YOUR WORD IS EVERYTHING

One of my favorite mentors, Kevin, taught me to always be honest in my commitments. Essentially, if you promise to do something, do it. No excuses.

As a startup business owner, with little experience under your belt, you can build a strong reputation simply by delivering on your word. Rather than overpromising and under-delivering, just agree to do what you know you're capable of and then knock it out of the park.

You deliver on time. You deliver with excellence. And you might even over-deliver and surprise your client. Yeah, girl!

Think about the times someone has let you down by not keeping her word — whether it was something seemingly innocent, like a supplier showing up 25 minutes late to your dinner meeting while you sat, impatiently, drinking alone; or whether it was the printer taking two days longer than expected, so you had no business cards for your networking event. How did it make you feel? Did you want to give her your return business? Probably not.

If you find yourself in a position where you can't deliver on time or as committed, 'fess up right away. Call your client and present your revised plan of action. Keep the communication open, honest, and upfront.

Be accountable and keep your word!

ASK FOR WHAT YOU WANT

No matter how far-fetched or ludicrous you think your request may sound, ask for it anyway. You will never know what a person is willing to agree to unless you make the ask.

Don't play it small.

Do you think Oprah got to where she is today because she asked for less than what she wanted? Or what about fashion designer Tory Burch? Or real estate mogul Barbara Corcoran?

These inspirational female entrepreneurs played big and won big. They asked for what they wanted. And if they were told no, they just moved the heck on.

The truth is you're going to be told no thousands of times in your lifetime. So get used to it. And remember that every "no" puts you closer to a "yes."

Ask for what you want.

PUT AN END TO POINTLESS APOLOGIES

All too often I hear women say things like "I'm sorry to bother you, but could I…?" or "I'm sorry to ask you this, but do you mind if…?"

How does it sound to you when you read those questions aloud? Because to me, it sounds insane and powerless. Why do we feel the need to apologize before making a simple ask? Are we actually bothering people by asking them a question? Furthermore, do you ever hear guys start sentences with these same words?

The words "I'm sorry" are incredibly powerful when delivered from the heart in the right circumstance. If I've done something wrong, I owe you an apology. If I've hurt your feelings, I should say I'm sorry. If I've made a big mistake that's caused you harm, I should apologize.

Eliminate these filler words from your professional dealings and just make the ask. You'll come across as the confident, powerful boss lady you are.

YOU'RE GOING TO GET A LOT OF NO'S

No. Not yet. Not now. Not ever.

Putting yourself and your business out there is necessary. You have to make the pitch, but not everyone is going to want what you're selling. Rejection is simply part of the entrepreneurial journey.

In the beginning, the noes feel a bit like a dagger through your heart. You're so excited for what you've created that you want everyone else to join in on the fun. So it's easy to take the rejection personally.

I used to stay up all night replaying meetings and wondering what I could have done to have gotten a yes out of a potential client. Nowadays, I just move on. There are other people who will want what I'm selling, and it's my job to find those people.

Just keep at it. Over time the noes don't feel so dramatic.

Barbara Corcoran, real-estate mogul and "Shark Tank" investor, says, "All the best things that happened to me happened after I was rejected. I knew the power of getting past no."

Take feedback from your customers, refine your sales strategy, and improve your pitch. With a little persistence, perseverance and patience, you'll be on your way.

ASK FOR WHAT YOU ARE WORTH

As new business owners we often think we can't charge top rate for our products or services because of a lack of time in business.

Wrong.

Charge what your products or services are worth 100% of the time.

First, what is the competitive landscape? When you look at similar businesses, what are they charging for like products and services?

Second, what margin is acceptable or standard for your industry? This is especially important if you're in a product-based business.

Next, what do you need to earn to be profitable? What's your break-even point?

Lastly, how much do you want to make? It's so important to have a stretch goal here, because it's simply not enough to just break even. You didn't become an entrepreneur because you wanted to scrape by for the rest of your life. You're a badass business owner who's a profit-driving machine! So set a BHAG (Big, Hairy, Audacious Goal) and go after it.

It's also important for the long-term health of your business that you don't rely on pricing alone. Price is a marketing lever, and an effective one at that, but it affects how people see your business. If you're asking for a low price or constantly discounting, people will perceive your company as having a lower value. Lower pricing erodes brand equity and strength.

For an easy example of this, think about Coke versus a generic cola brand. Coke charges a premium for its product, its branding is on point, and customers are willing to pay for it.

The generic cola brand sells on price, and price alone. It sells to those who are price-sensitive, but it will never be able to raise its price to Coke levels.

If you sell for less now, you devalue yourself and your product. It will be nearly impossible later to raise prices if your perceived brand equity is low.

So ask for your worth! You are worth it.

YOU
ARE CAPABLE OF
AMAZING
THINGS

DON'T OVERSELL

There's nothing that ruins a sale like a good case of verbal diarrhea. You know, the salesperson who doesn't know when to shut up and just keeps spewing the benefits of the product, while the buyer sits there in silence unable to get a word in edgewise.

This occurs in live sales pitches, emails, phone calls, voicemails, marketing materials, collateral, retail stores, and more! I see and hear it every single day.

On the whole, buyers know what they want. They're smart and savvy. If they need more information they're going to ask. So it's your job, as a salesperson for your company, to present a solid pitch and then shut up.

We need to give our target customers just enough information to make an informed decision but not so much that we overload them with meaningless words, content, and chatter.

Make it succinct and easy for your customer to say yes.

DON'T KNOW THE ANSWER, DON'T MAKE IT UP

You know the scenario. You're about to make a big sale and the client suddenly stumps you with a question you really don't know how to answer. You want the sale so badly that you consider making up an answer just to close the deal.

Before that lie leaves your lips, take a pause. It can be so tempting to make up a response, especially as early entrepreneurs because we're still trying to "prove" ourselves. We're trying to prove ourselves not only to our clients, but also to ourselves. We want to know we're capable of running the business and haven't gotten in over our head.

The best response is always an honest one. Let the client know that you need to do a little research and commit to getting them an answer right away. Then, get your butt back to the office and figure it out. Follow up with your client and give the client the right answer, not some fabricated story you'll have to dig yourself out of later.

Honesty and transparency will set you a mile apart from your competitors, boss babe.

BUTTON IT UP

'm talking about crossing the t's and dotting the i's. I'm a huge believer in making it official with paperwork.

When you're on the buying side, ask for written estimates of work. Make sure it's completely clear what you're getting for your money and when they expect you to pay.

When you're on the selling side, insist that your clients sign a contract, scope of work agreement, or purchase order. Make sure it's clear exactly what you're providing and the terms of their payment to you.

A consulting client of mine recently revealed that she never has her clients sign a scope of work. She went on to say that she's struggling with clients sending her requests to complete projects she feels are beyond what "she should be doing." And herein lies the problem. She and her clients aren't on the same page because the terms of their engagement aren't clear.

It's time to put an end to handshake deals. Be clear from the beginning on the terms of the agreement, and formalize it with paperwork.

Contracts aren't meant to make things more complicated; they serve to do just the opposite. They protect both the buyer and the seller by making known exactly what both parties have agreed to.

Just do it, because I can guarantee you one day you'll be thankful you did.

BE NIMBLE

In our fast-paced digital world, we've become accustomed to having everything we want at our fingertips within just minutes.

So it stands to reason that your own customers and clients will expect the same. This is when it pays to be quick on your feet.

Reply to incoming emails and requests promptly. Make decisions swiftly and with conviction. Be the first to acknowledge a mistake, and quickly rectify the situation. Change course when necessary and do so without complaints.

Being nimble sets you apart from your competition. If you're reliable, swift to answer and accountable to your word, you will come out ahead every time.

PEN, PAPER, AND A STAMP

I'm going to ask you to get really old-school right now.

The next time you have the opportunity to express gratitude, dig out the pen and paper and write a handwritten thank-you. This simple gesture will wow your customers, clients and teammates. Every. Single. Time.

In the era of excessive emails, you can stand out from the crowd by showing someone you cared enough to spend five minutes putting the pen to paper.

I've received countless compliments over the years for taking the time to send a little snail mail. My friend Ashley likes to call it "sending a happy," because it's always such a nice surprise these days to find something in your mailbox that's not a bill.

Give postcards a try, too. I like to send them to top clients when I'm on the road for work or fun. It's a nice way to show people you're thinking of them.

LOCATION, LOCATION, LOCATION

Have you ever found yourself in a coffee shop, eavesdropping on the conversation at the table next to you? Personally, this is one of my favorite guilty pleasures.

But it proves it's all too easy for other people to overhear what's going on when you meet in a public place. And it's a small world. I've overheard complete strangers talking in public about people and businesses I know, with intimate details.

When you're setting up meetings with clients or business partners, consider the context of the meeting so you can choose a location wisely. Coffee and lunch dates are not always appropriate.

Sometimes a casual meeting at a coffee shop is just what's in order. I love grabbing a cafe Americano with a new acquaintance so we can get to know each other. Lunch dates or happy hour can be great as well, as long as nothing confidential or otherwise "touchy" needs to be discussed.

But sometimes you need to get down to brass tacks. You need to negotiate. You need to pitch your business. You need to have a conversation you don't want the entire coffee shop eavesdropping on. So schedule those meetings in private. Meet at your office or theirs. And if you don't have an office, check into co-working spaces or hotels where meeting rooms are available by the hour.

Set yourself up for success and choose a location that's just the right fit!

DON'T SPILL YOUR BEANS

I made the mistake once of telling a business idea to someone who I thought was my friend. Five months later, he brought my business idea to market. I could have died.

I was so excited the day I met him, and I really thought we were sharing stories openly, simply as friends and supporters of each other as entrepreneurs. I was dead wrong.

If you're working on a new idea for your business, be cautious about the people with whom you share that information. Your good idea can become someone else's business plan in a matter of minutes. People can — and do — steal ideas, especially within an industry.

It can be hard to know whom to trust, especially when you're a young entrepreneur who's still learning the ropes and making connections in your industry. So use caution. Keep your valuable business ideas in the vault while you're working on bringing them to market, so you don't accidentally give a competitor the chance the jump in.

PEOPLE CAN BE NOSY

I often get asked, "How do you make money?" or "How much money does that make?" and I return the favor by asking, "What is your salary?" A bit hostile, maybe, but it seems to put an end to the conversation.

Sometimes well-intentioned people can't fathom how we've created a business from scratch and made it profitable. It's so outside of their realm of understanding that it drives them to ask questions that are clearly inappropriate.

You are never obligated to answer these types of questions, unless it's to the IRS, I suppose. So you may choose a more polite response, such as "That's not information I share publicly," and then change the subject.

DO WHAT YOU GOTTA DO, GIRL

As an early entrepreneur, it may be necessary to supplement your income. If you find yourself in this position, I don't want you to feel guilty or ashamed for one second!

Some entrepreneurs are fortunate enough to launch their business while they're still employed and bringing in a steady paycheck. It's an incredible blessing to have this kind of opportunity to start growing your business before you take the proverbial leap.

However, for many of us, the story sounds more like, "I took the leap and then I had to backtrack to get a job just to pay my bills." This was part of my story, and it was something I felt really embarrassed about — until one conversation completely changed my perspective.

I was introduced by a former co-worker to a woman named Grace. He thought we should meet because we both owned similar businesses, though she had been running hers for over a decade. Her event firm produced music events across the country, and after talking to her for just 10 minutes I was completely enamored of her. She was so insightful and positive, and it was refreshing to meet someone who had been there, done that, and lived to tell the tale.

I was peppering her with questions about how she got started in the business, lessons she'd learned about our industry, and how long I should expect it to take to turn a profit. I told her I was really struggling to get through the first year because we weren't in the black like I'd hoped, and my forecast was way off on revenues and expenses. She understood, and we shared some laughs about how challenging the early years can be.

She then told me that during her startup, she ended up taking a part-time job booking bands for a restaurant client. "I didn't want to do it, but I had to do it just to pay my bills. I needed to take the edge off financially, so I could keep plugging away on my company. I just had to get my own ego out of the way."

Her story hit home. I desperately needed to supplement my income, but I was letting my own ego and feelings about what others would think stand in my way.

The day after I met with Grace, I started picking up part-time work. I walked dogs for friends, I picked up catering shifts, I taught yoga classes anywhere I could. I started earning money to offset my living expenses.

Through her story, Grace gave me permission to not see myself as a failure for needing to supplement my income. I was able to reframe my thinking that this was just a step in the bigger journey, a step that afforded me the ability to keep plugging away at my dreams.

So do what you gotta do, girl. You are not alone.

EMBRACE YOUR JOURNEY

LIVE LEAN

When you're in the startup phase, it's important to learn to live on less, personally and professionally. The first few years of owning a business are challenging, and finances will likely be at the top of the "pain in the ass" list.

You'll learn that things cost more than you estimated. Or that it's taking longer than you'd hoped to bring in a big paycheck. So while you're learning the ropes and building your business, keep a light financial footprint at home and at work. The less unnecessary overhead you have, the easier you'll sleep at night while you're figuring it all out.

Start looking at essentials vs. nonessentials. Is it necessary that you have cable TV? Probably not. Do you have to get your nails done every week? Nope. Could you buy a generic version of Tylenol? Absolutely. Can you give up that $4 latte, even half of the week? Darn right. Do you really need that 12th pair of jeans? Seriously?!

What about at the office? Can you stop printing presentations and go digital instead? Yes! Do you need to buy the upgraded version of your accounting software? Eh, it can probably wait. Could you skip a lunch out and instead brown bag it to work? Yeah, totally. Is now the time to upgrade your laptop? Not unless it's about to give you the blue screen of death!

Little savings add up, and it can make a huge difference in the early years as you're growing a financially viable and stable business. Learn to live lean early on and you'll be well on your way to financial freedom before you know it!

GET YOUR FINANCES IN ORDER

f you're going to run a rock-star business, it's time to start acting like a pro in the finance department. Whether you're handling your own accounting or you hire a bookkeeper to assist, let's just hit upon a few basics you need to have in place.

Create a separate bank account for all things business. I'm constantly blown away by the number of entrepreneurs who are running their finances out of their personal bank account. Get it separate so you can track the financial health of your business, independent of your personal finances.

If you're using a personal credit card for your company, I recommend dedicating one card specifically for business expenses. It makes month-end reconciliation and processing so much easier when you know that every expense on that one statement is associated with your business, versus having to review every line and separate personal from professional.

Adopt an accounting system or software to track your finances. You want to be able to send invoices to customers, track the status of incoming payments, and capture outgoing payments to your suppliers.

QuickBooks is a fairly common option, and one I've used, but there are dozens of other software and cloud-based solutions available. So do a little research and decide what you need for your business.

Not only will you be able to see a snapshot of how your business is performing on any given day, it also makes tax time a cinch when you can just turn the files over to your accountant to complete your business return.

Finances don't have to be panic-inducing! This is one area for which hiring some outsourced help may be necessary and super-beneficial. So if that is the route you need to take to keep some sanity, don't feel bad for one minute.

BUDGET LIKE A BOSS

Rock-star business owners know what's going on with their finances at any given moment. You should too.

This doesn't need to be anything fancy. You can use a simple spreadsheet to track what's coming in and what's going out. But of course, if you have an accounting software or service you prefer to use, go for it.

Every year I like to create an "original budget," my estimate of what I think it will cost me to run my business (expenses) and what I think I'll bring in (revenue). I calculate the difference (revenue minus expenses) and it gives me my net profit estimate. Easy breezy.

Then I create a version of the same budget that's my "rolling budget," where I start replacing the estimated values with actual values as they come in. I update my budget at least once a month, but you may find doing this every one to two weeks more helpful.

This file ultimately becomes the "final budget," which is my year-end calculation of how it all panned out. It makes it easy to quickly compare your final figures to your estimate, to see how your company performed. It will also give great insight into how well you budgeted at the beginning of the year.

As you repeat this process annually, you'll be able to see trends in how your business is performing. It's powerful information that every boss should have at her fingertips. Don't hesitate to ask for help, though, if numbers just aren't your thing. A good bookkeeper or accountant should be able to get you on the right path.

THINGS WILL COST MORE THAN YOU THOUGHT

You developed a kickass annual budget, because that's what all awesome business owners do. You even put in a buffer for some expenses that you thought might come in higher. Yet here you are, paying an invoice for an unbudgeted expense that came completely out of left field!

Unfortunately, this is the nature of the beast. Even the best forecasters in the world will get it wrong sometimes, because we simply can't know 100% of what the future holds. And stuff happens, like your computer dying out of the blue.

So how is a boss lady to deal with these financial land mines?

Set aside a savings stash and have a line of credit ready to deploy for emergencies. Common advice for personal savings is to have three to six months' worth of living expenses in a savings account. For your business, it may range from three months to a year's worth of operating expenses.

Don't freak if you don't have that on hand right now. Start saving today!

THINGS WILL TAKE LONGER THAN YOU THOUGHT

Not only do projects often cost more than you originally anticipated, but those same projects will take longer than you expected to complete. It's the classic double punch!

As a person who lives and dies by her calendar, I can tell you I struggle with this every single day. I hate when projects run long, and yet I often am part of the reason for the delay.

Even with a killer project timeline, precise deliverables, deadlines, and an accountable team, things may not go according to plan. Some projects just take more hours to complete than you estimated, so that requires adjusting your own expectations.

Sometimes your employees or outsourced suppliers aren't prioritizing the right work, so that requires firm project management and communication of expectations. Sometimes an employee is out sick for a week, so that requires patience or jumping in to complete her work. Sometimes you just want to take a vacation, and you push your own timeline back for some much-needed downtime.

Bottom line, there are a million reasons your work may not be happening according to plan, but being clear with your expectations and deadlines is a must.

Build the plan. Work the plan. Hold yourself and your team accountable and adjust as needed. You'll get it done, boss lady!

WHERE DID MY SAVINGS GO

Your savings account may take a beating during the startup phase. Mine did. In fact, I'd say mine underwent destruction and annihilation before I was able to rebuild.

The reality is I way overestimated my income and underestimated by expenses in my first year of business. I even thought I was being conservative in my estimate, yet I still got my ass handed to me.

I'm not alone in this story. The vast majority of entrepreneurs I meet tell similar tales of digging deep into their savings just to stay above water, often taking on part-time jobs to help fuel the pursuit of their business. Some girls end up moving back in with their parents or taking on multiple roommates to bring down expenses.

It's important to hear this stuff for these reasons:

- The life of an entrepreneur is not always glamorous.
- The startup phase is notoriously tough and requires a lot of grit to survive.
- You're not alone. I've been there and so have thousands of other women before you.

You can survive this. Save when you can. Learn to live on less. Don't spend it until you earn it. Supplement your income. Do what you've gotta do, girlfriend. I've got a high-five right here waiting for you.

NOT ALL MONEY IS GOOD MONEY

It can be tempting to take on every client or customer that comes your way, especially in the early days when cash flow can be a challenge. But not all money is created equal.

Sometimes clients are not a good fit. They may not mesh with your company or team culturally, or you may just not like working with them.

Other times the project is wrong. It may be outside the scope of your business, or it may require you to invest in capabilities, infrastructure or equipment that you're not ready for.

Give it a little gut check. Are you excited to take on the new work? Does the project fit within your company mission and vision? If the answer to both of these is no, politely pass. It may end up saving you a lot of headache in the long run.

INSURE YOUR ASS

I'm going to sound like your mom for a moment, but this is something you should take really seriously. You need insurance.

Get health insurance. Yeah, paying for your own health insurance sucks versus having your employer pay for it. But if you become sick or injured, you'll rest a lot easier at night knowing your health insurance is there. Self-care is extremely important as you take the helm of your business, because if you're not working, you might not be bringing home a paycheck.

Get business insurance. Virtually all businesses should carry a general liability policy, but depending on your industry and scope of work, you may need other coverage, such as errors and omissions, workers' compensation, etc.

Ask your entrepreneur friends to recommend knowledgeable agents who specialize in business coverage. Interview at least three insurance agents to get a recommendation for coverage and a quote. Choose the best coverage for your business and be sure to review and update the policy annually, as your business changes.

While every entrepreneur hopes the worst-case scenario doesn't occur, if bad luck does befall you, you'll be glad your insurance policy is there to kick in.

PROTECT YOUR STUFF

You've put a lot of hard work into creating your business and its products and services. Now it's time to protect them.

Let's cover the basics.

You need to create a legal business entity for your company. This could be an LLC, a C corporation, an S corp, a partnership or a sole proprietorship, among others. A good business attorney or accountant can help advise you of the best structure for your business, which ultimately can help protect your personal assets versus the business's debts.

You may also need a trademark. This is all about protecting your brand from potential competitors in the market. You can trademark the name and logo of your company, product, or service. The more unique the better, and the more easily enforceable.

Patents are another form of protection for intellectual property. If you invent a product, you likely will pursue a patent to make sure no other company enters the marketplace trying to copy and sell your invention.

These things are really the un-sexy side of business, but they're incredibly important for the health of your company. I encourage you to find a good lawyer and accountant to advise you in these matters so you can make a smart decision for your business.

BRAND THYSELF

You might not have graduated with a degree in marketing, but that shouldn't prevent you from developing a strong brand presence for your company.

Creating a brand is all about establishing a cohesive look and feel in your marketing materials so that you become easily recognizable to your customers. Fear not: You can do it!

Most businesses start with logo design. This one element will be used time and time again to represent your business in a snapshot. Remember, you're designing a logo that should resonate with and appeal to your avatar and target market. You're not just trying to create something "cool."

I recommend you hire a designer to create your logo, versus trying to do it on your own. (That is, unless you're in the business of graphic design!) The quality, or lack thereof, always shows. One great resource for developing a logo on a budget is 99Designs.com. It's how the Hatch Tribe logo came to be. You can submit a proposal for your project, and dozens of designers will create options from which you can choose. If you don't love any of the options, you don't pay. It's that simple.

With your logo in hand, make some decisions about the color palette you'll use on your marketing materials. I suggest choosing three to four colors that complement your logo. Google "Adobe Color Wheel" and you'll find a really cool website with hundreds of color palette ideas.

Then take a look at fonts. It's wise to select one to two fonts that you'll stick with on everything you do. You might choose a font for headlines and a different font for body copy. Ideally these fonts are readily available, like in Word, so that you can use them across various types of communication for your business. And don't ever choose Comic Sans. Ever.

Now land that marketing message by thinking through your brand voice. If your brand were a person, who would she be? What does she sound like when she's talking to your avatar?

Landing your brand doesn't have to be overly complicated. It really just takes consistency, coupled with an understanding of your target consumer. You'll likely tweak things over time as you learn more about your business and customers, and that's awesome!

PICK YOUR PLATFORM

Social media is awesome for marketing, but it's impossible to be everywhere at once and do so with excellence and authenticity. And today we have so many options for social media that it's a bit overwhelming.

Now is the time to pick your platform.

Where are your customers hanging out? Do they live on Facebook, but can't even tell you what Snapchat is? Are they on the go and only have time for Twitter? Do they love watching your YouTube tutorials?

Pick the top two to three platforms where your customer is engaged on the reg, and own those. Create a content calendar for each platform and post there regularly. Be sure to interact with your fans — they'll love it!

The key is to be consistent and authentic, and to speak to your ideal customer in her language on the platforms she (not you) loves most.

BACK THAT THING UP

We're in the digital era now, doll, and you have created some important stuff you can't afford to lose.

Whether it's the latest version of your business plan or the new product shots for your fall line, so much of your work will be living and breathing on your computer. And digital devices do fail from time to time.

Invest in a service such as Carbonite to back up all your team's files, for every single computer and hard drive.

It's a small investment that could literally save your business. Spend the money.

WHICH WAY

We live in a world of endless choice, which can be both a blessing and a curse.

As a budding entrepreneur, you will have thousands of choices in front of you. Sometimes you'll make great decisions and they will lead you down a wonderful path. Other times you'll make a bad call and you'll pay the price. But don't beat yourself up when this happens.

This is just part of the learning process. As a startup entrepreneur, you're navigating a world of unknowns. Presumably you've never owned a business before this, so there are some lessons you just couldn't know until you experienced them firsthand. I like to say, "You can't know what you don't know, until you've done it."

Every choice you make, regardless of the outcome, helps you learn. So if you choose Road A, but then wish you'd chosen Road B, change course and move on.

You're building a lifetime of lessons that will make you a better-informed entrepreneur and one hell of human being.

"IF IT'S BOTH
TERRIFYING
AND AMAZING
THEN YOU SHOULD
DEFINITELY PURSUE IT."

— ERADA SVETLANA

TRUST YOUR GUT

When you're facing a big decision in life or business, it sometimes comes down to a little bit of magic. We lean on our intellect to help guide us to the "smart" decision. We lean on our heart to help guide us to something that "feels good." But our head and our heart alone don't always give us the "right" answer.

It's time for a gut check. This is where your intuition reigns supreme. Listen in to the feelings below the surface. When you think of the possible outcomes, how do they make you feel? Excited? Nervous? Dread-filled? Passionate? Energetic?

When I talk to my clients about times they've had to lean on their intuition to make a decision, they often describe it as a feeling of "just knowing." Oh, how I wish it were more scientific than that. But I think the truth is when you know, you know.

Trusting your gut is a skill that will develop over time. So just keep listening. Allow yourself to pick up that small whisper deep in your soul, because it just might be the most important words uttered, if only you're receptive enough to hear them.

One of the most meaningful quotes I've heard on this topic is from Oprah. I hope you'll hear her words in your heart when you need them most:

"The only time I've ever made mistakes is when I didn't listen. So what I know is, God is love and God is life, and your life is always speaking to you. First in whispers. ... It's subtle, those whispers. And if you don't pay attention to the whispers, it gets louder and louder. It's like getting thumped upside the head, like my grandmother used to do. ... You don't pay attention to that, it's like getting a brick upside your head. You don't pay attention to that, the whole brick wall falls down. That's the pattern I've seen in my life, and it's played out over and over again on this show."

INSPIRATION COMES
FROM ALL PLACES

Take a few steps outside of your regular, routine path in life, and there are hundreds of things that can spark inspiration for your business. It's the joy of living in a world where cultures are vast, exploration is easy, and diversity of thought and creation is abundant.

Let's say you're a chef. If you only ever go to other restaurants to find inspiration for your business, you're only pulling from within one circle of influence. But if you step just beyond the circle, there are a wealth of other places to find inspiration: a local produce farm, a heritage-breed pig farmer, a century-old vineyard, a home-cooked meal served by your grandmother, a small-town farmers market, or a trip to abroad to see the fish market where the fresh catch is dragged in daily.

Inspiration comes from everywhere. Ideas are often sparked just by exposing ourselves to new places and things. You never know when the next big idea for your business is going to hit you, but in my experience it often seems to happen after I've been exposed to something new.

Live a life of full of exploration. Go see stuff. Go do the amazing things that sit just beyond your comfort zone. Seek new experiences, even in your own hometown. Broaden your horizons and you'll expand the limits of what you thought possible for your business.

BECOME A SPONGE

Make it your mission to learn from the best and brightest entrepreneurs and businesspeople. Sometimes they're these mega superstar entrepreneurs or companies that everyone aspires to become; often they're just the girl next door who created something from nothing and is chock-full of wisdom to impart.

Whether you pick up their book, tune in to their weekly podcast, or meet up with them in person, soak up the lessons that you can apply to your business. Sometimes it's just the smallest tidbit of information, often said in passing, that will leave an indelible impact on your thinking for the rest of your life.

Years ago, when I was working in a corporate job, I had an incredible manager named Sean. He was the type of person who would push you as an employee to be nothing short of excellent, but he also took great interest in your well-being. That's to say he cared deeply about us, personally and professionally.

One particular year we were facing dramatic cutbacks in our marketing budgets. My co-workers and I were very vocal about how we didn't think we were going to be able to deliver our sales goals in light of losing nearly 50% of our marketing investment. After allowing us to complain for 15 to 20 minutes, Sean silenced the room, and with a completely calm voice he said, "Guys, it is what it is. Let's move on."

And we shut up. And we moved on.

To this day, that one little tidbit has stuck in my head and replayed time and again when a challenging, yet unavoidable circumstance has presented itself. I learned that there was, in fact, no use in crying over spilt milk and that moving on is often the only course of action.

I've gleaned countless other pieces of wisdom over time simply by surrounding myself with incredibly talented and experienced people.

You are never too old to learn, and I'd argue that one of the keys to entrepreneurial success is constantly improving your knowledge. So soak it up, sister. You don't have to agree with everything a person says, but I believe that every person has at least one incredible lesson they can impart.

LISTEN UP

I am a podcast junkie. I love, love, love listening to podcasts, and here's why you should, too.

One, they're a wealth of information. There are podcasts available on virtually any topic you can dream up, such as being an entrepreneur, thriving as a woman in business, mastering marketing skills, and industry-specific endeavors.

Two, they're often hosted by the top minds in business. If you want to learn from the best of the best, you can! Some of the brightest minds from around the globe are dispensing their knowledge and life lessons via their podcasts.

Three, they're free. So you get a wealth of information from the brightest minds in your industry, and it doesn't cost you a dime. Score!

Lastly, it's available on the go. So while you're driving to a meeting or getting in 30 minutes on the treadmill, you can be expanding your mind. Portable learning is awesome for the busy gal who doesn't always have time to read lengthy books or watch hours of video training.

A few podcasts that I love and recommend are: EOFire (John Lee Dumas), Online Marketing Made Easy (Amy Porterfield), Smart Passive Income (Pat Flynn), Good Life Project (Jonathan Fields), #girlboss Radio (Sophia Amoruso). Check them out, and find a few of your own!

ENCOURAGEMENT ROCKS

People will be curious about your story. They'll want to know all about what it took for you to open a business, how you got over your fear of failure, and what life is actually like on the other side.

Why? Because chances are the woman you're speaking with has a dream inside her own heart, and she's just too scared to take that giant leap.

When I meet a budding entrepreneur, I remind myself that encouragement means the world coming from someone who's been there, done that. Think back to those people who rooted for you. They told you that you could do it, that you'd land on your feet even if you failed, and that you could always go back to "doing what you did before" as a last resort.

They helped you get to a yes!

This type of encouragement makes a world of difference.

IT GETS EASIER, BUT...

The first few years of business can feel like an endless uphill battle. You're trying to figure out how to do everything: run a business, manage workloads, hire people, find new clients, and a litany of other big and little things that you never had to deal with working for someone else.

You're literally learning and growing every minute of the day, which can leave you wondering whether you're ever going to feel like you've "got it."

The answer is "yes, and no."

Yes, you will become more confident as an entrepreneur. It will begin to feel easier as you acquire more knowledge and experience. It just takes time.

And no, you will never totally have it mastered. But that's just because the world is complex and ever-changing. Just when you think you have it figured out, life will throw you a curveball that can change the course of your business, sometimes overnight.

So get yourself a little persistence, perseverance and patience. You're in this for the long haul, girlfriend.

YOU'RE CAPABLE OF GREATNESS

Every day I hear stories of humans doing extraordinary things. Eleanor Cunningham goes skydiving for the first time on her 100th birthday just because it was on her "bucket list."

Laura Dekker sets sail to circumnavigate the globe solo at age 14. She completes the journey two years later at age 16, making her the youngest person ever to complete the feat.

Mo'ne Davis challenges the status quo by becoming, at age 13, the first girl in Little League World Series history to earn a win and pitch a shutout.

Twenty-six-year-old Lauren Bush Lauren founds the organization FEED to fight global hunger. Since its inception in 2007, FEED has provided more than 94 million meals to people around the world.

Melissa Ben-Ishay gets fired from her advertising job in 2008 and decides to just do what she loves — bake cupcakes. During the eight years that follow, her passion project turns into a 13-store mini-cupcake empire, Baked by Melissa.

In 2016, Hillary Clinton becomes the first female presidential nominee in United States history.

Malala Yousafzai was shot in the head by a Taliban gunman after defying cultural norms and demanding girls be allowed to receive education. She survived and went on to receive the Nobel Peace Prize, and she is now a leading children and women's rights activist at the age of 19.

What do all these stories have in common? Sure, they're all women and they've accomplished some pretty incredible things. But what ultimately unites them is that they took action. They had dreams and visions of what was possible, and they pursued them one step at a time.

Within you is that same seed of possibility. You are capable of greatness, just as thousands of women who have come before you. Commit to pursuing your dream and becoming a doer. It's by taking action that dreams become reality. I believe in you, and you should, too.

PURSUE YOUR VISION AND MISSION RELENTLESSLY

As the HBIC (Head Bitch in Charge!), it's your job to make sure your business is growing in alignment with your vision and mission. Keep the picture of your ideal company in your heart and mind and go after it. Every. Single. Day.

Staying true to the heart of what you wanted to create in the first place is so important. It helps guide everyday decision-making so you can build a business that you'll love, one that your customers will adore, and one that contributes to the world in a meaningful way.

As you grow your business, your vision and mission will likely evolve. You'll learn more every single year about what you do well, what you don't, and the work that you truly enjoy. As new team members join your crew, they will also contribute to the picture, allowing you to see a future you never would have dreamed possible. Let the experiences unfold and inform your vision and mission as you grow.

If you feel the direction of your company has gone astray, go back to your original company vision and mission, and steer the ship back on course. You're one hell of a captain, sister!

IMAGINE IT AS SO

When elite athletes are interviewed about how they've risen to the top of their sport, many will say they visualize themselves winning. They mentally play the game, practice the moves they'll make, and picture themselves scoring that winning goal.

Similarly, imagination and vision play a big role in the startup entrepreneur's belief in achieving success. If you're able to see yourself running your company and becoming a wild success, you're creating a vision in your mind's eye that can be pursued. Visualization techniques are powerful tools for achieving any big dream. Give it a try!

COMPARISON IS THE
THIEF OF JOY

t's only human to look at your peers to see how you "stack up." So occasionally you may find yourself comparing your business and journey to that of another entrepreneur.

How did she grow her company so fast? How did she get funding before me? Why does she keep getting these big clients? How did she make a million dollars? What am I doing wrong? Why am I not as successful as her yet?

All this thinking and comparing serves little purpose, other than to make you feel resentful and crazy. It sends you into a spiral of comparison that ends up leaving you feeling terrible about yourself.

As Sofia Amoruso, author of #bossbabe and founder of NastyGal says: "Don't compare your hustle to their highlight reel." And that's the truth.

You can never really know the whole story of what someone has done to get to where they are. And every one of us has taken a unique road to our current state of business.

Comparison robs you of the ability to feel joy about your own story and experience. I'd encourage you to instead feel proud of what your sisters are accomplishing and for the successes they're having. You, too, are just as worthy and capable of those big wins.

If they've done it, so can you! That's a comparison worth making.

EMPOWER
THE WOMEN
AROUND YOU

CONFIDENCE CAN COME
FROM ANYWHERE

About a year ago, I took up running after a long hiatus. Even though I had once completed a marathon (mostly out of sheer determination), I was never much of a runner. I was the girl who struggled along at a 12-minute mile and occasionally sped it up to a 10-minute mile. A speed runner, I was not.

Over the past year, I've become a much better runner. I slowly and steadily increased my pace. It became a bit of game because I wanted to see how quickly I could run three miles.

One day, much to my surprise, I realized that I had run at a 9-minute-mile pace. So I kept pushing it, until I recently hit a personal best. I ran three miles in 23:40, for an average 7:53 pace. I was ecstatic.

I kept pushing the limits of what I thought was possible, and with every incremental improvement in speed, my confidence soared.

My point in telling you this is that my confidence boost didn't just stop with running. It had this amazing halo effect on the rest of my life and my belief in my own abilities.

It's given me real-life experience that shows that when I set a goal, stick to it, and pursue it with everything I've got, I will see growth. It's allowed me to show up at work and believe that I am capable of things well beyond what my mind allows me to believe.

I encourage you to find opportunities that challenge you out-side of work. Use them as confidence builders, because that halo effect is something fierce!

MAKE SOMEONE'S DAY

want you to WOW someone today. It could be a customer, a client, a teammate, or a fellow entrepreneur. Just choose someone and figure out how you can surprise and delight him or her.

When I was in the beer business we employed this model at local bars and restaurants. We'd find someone who was already enjoying our brand of beer, and we'd surprise them by delivering a few rounds of beer. Then we'd delight them by picking up their entire tab. These unsuspecting beer drinkers would be completely shocked, and they'd often be so grateful you'd receive far more hugs than you'd ever imagine. We created brand-loyal enthusiasts for life.

Consider your business and how you can uniquely surprise and delight this person. Perhaps you reward an employee with an extra half-day away from the office and give her 40 bucks to go get a mani-pedi. Or you sneak a free shirt into your customer's bag with a handwritten note that she'll find when she gets home. Or you stop by your client's office and drop off a vase of freshly cut flowers from your garden and a cinnamon roll you baked that morning, just because you can.

It's really such a joy to give joy to others. It makes you feel good in the process, similar to the afterglow people report after volunteering for a cause. And it may just endear you to a customer for life.

Have some fun with it! I can't wait to see what you do.

BE GRATEFUL

Gratitude is all the rage these days, and I'd say that's a great thing for society. Everywhere you turn, there are books about gratitude, jewelry that reminds us to be grateful, and thousands of inspirational quotes about giving thanks in our daily lives.

But the truth is, it's easy to get caught up in the things that aren't going our way. We're prone to seeing and dwelling on what's not working.

Case in point: I could have a hugely successful event for thousands of people, but the two negative reviews I received on social media will be stuck in my head for weeks. I'll replay them over and over and make myself mad thinking about what I could have done differently.

It's the human condition, but that doesn't mean we're destined for a life of gloom and negativity.

Simple shifts in thinking can have an epic impact on our overall well-being. Being grateful is one of those practices. When we learn to be thankful for our big and little successes, we leave way less room for doubt, fear, and anxiety to creep in.

My best tool for this is a gratitude journal. As you're settling in for the evening, I want you to reflect on what you're grateful for in three key areas: work, life, and myself. Write down at least one thing for each category. For example:

- Work: I'm grateful for bringing on a new client this week.
- Life: I'm grateful for my boyfriend, who's been cheering me on. He's my rock!
- Myself: I'm grateful for my work ethic, which allowed me to power through midnight last night to get that sales pitch done.

It doesn't matter how big or small, as it's really about cultivating an attitude of thankfulness. When you're having a tough day, forcing yourself to shift your focus to gratitude can be so powerful. It's also amazing to re-read the things you wrote days, weeks, and months ago. It will give you a jolt of motivation just when you need it most.

PAY IT FORWARD

One of the most meaningful ways you can contribute to the entrepreneur community is through mentoring. No matter how old you are or how long you've been in business, you have the ability to mentor someone. Within you is a unique set of experiences and abilities that will be of value to another person, even if it's just knowing how to show up and listen.

Make it a priority to invest your time, energy, and expertise in other women who are on the entrepreneurial journey. By doing so, we grow this community from within. We prove that we're better off together than we are apart. We insist that we cheer one another on, versus tearing each other down. We show that we're a powerful force to be reckoned with, by shattering age-old stereotypes about women in business and in life. We create a better future for generations of girls to come.

This is a legacy of which I hope you'll be proud to be a part, because you are part of the tribe now. Live it, breathe it, and nourish it.

CELEBRATE YOUR SUCCESS

It took me a long time to learn this lesson. As an entrepreneur, I tend to be super-critical of my own work and I don't always see the wins in what I'm doing and creating every day.

As Jaime Tardy of Eventual Millionaire says, "Success is a series of small wins." I came to realize this is spot-on.

When we're driving toward a big goal, such as launching a business or a new project, it can be tempting to focus only on the end goal. But it's those decisions and steps you take every single day that make it possible for you to become wildly successful over the long haul.

Create a culture in your business that celebrates all sizes of wins, whether that's landing a new client, finalizing the copy for your website, or surviving the first year of business. Break those bigger goals down into manageable steps, and make it a cause for celebrating when you reach them.

Celebrating successes, big and small, helps keep you and your team motivated. It builds a culture that rewards results. And, well, it's just a hell of a lot more fun.

Pass the cake, folks!

BE PROUD

Somewhere along the way, pride got a bad rap.

As little girls, many of us were raised to be humble about our accomplishments. It was as though being proud meant we were boasting or bragging or otherwise putting ourselves above others.

The essence of pride is quite different, so it's time to reframe this thinking.

The meaning of pride is "a feeling of deep pleasure or satisfaction derived from one's own achievements, or the achievements of those with whom one is closely associated."

That doesn't sound so crazy, does it?

You should be proud of what you're doing. You made the choice to follow your dreams. You leapt out of the comfort zone into the wild world of entrepreneurship. You took a chance that so few will ever dare to do. And you're out there making it happen every single day.

You should also be proud of your sisters and brothers on this journey. It's incredible to see the success of your peers and be able to feel a sense of pride for what they're accomplishing in their own lives.

Just because you're proud of yourself doesn't mean you're a bragging, boasting bitch. And if you are, stop it!

It's possible to be both proud and humble about your accomplishments. Give yourself permission to feel like the badass that you are!

YOU'RE DOING AN AMAZING JOB

High-five, girl. I am so proud of you for taking on this entrepreneurial journey.

Sending you a big ol' cosmic hug from across the globe.

XO

~ Hilary / Founder / Hatch Tribe

"THERE IS FREEDOM
WAITING FOR YOU,
ON THE BREEZES OF THE SKY,
AND YOU ASK
"WHAT IF I FALL?"
OH BUT MY DARLING,
**WHAT IF
YOU FLY?"**

— ERIN HANSON

HATCH TRIBE

WELCOME TO THE TRIBE

Join the movement to empower, cultivate and connect women entrepreneurs across the globe.

www.hatchtribe.com

44351938R00080

Made in the USA
Middletown, DE
04 June 2017